Best of Sedona Productions
P.O. Box 4326
Sedona, AZ 86340

Printed in the United States of America
First Printing, 2020

ISBN: 978-1-56457-000-0
ISBN:978-1-56457-001-7 (ebook)

Interior Design: Yvonne Stepanow
Cover Design: Joey Best

Best of Sedona Productions
P.O. Box 4326
Sedona, AZ 86340
www.healingpawsmethod.com

DISCLAIMER:

The publisher and the author are providing this book and its contents on an "as is" basis and make no representations or warranties of any kind with respect to this book or its contents. The publisher and the author disclaim all such representations and warranties, including but not limited to warranties of healthcare for a particular purpose. In addition, the publisher and the author assume no responsibility for errors, inaccuracies, omissions, or any other inconsistencies herein. The content of this book is for informational purposes only and is not intended to diagnose, treat, cure ,mitigate or prevent any condition or disease. You understand that this book is not intended as a substitute for consultation with a licensed veterinarian. Please consult with your own veterinarian or healthcare specialist regarding the suggestions and recommendations made in this book. The use of this book implies your acceptance of this disclaimer. The publisher and the author make no guarantees concerning the level of success you may experience by following the advice and methods contained in this book, and you accept the risk that results will differ for each individual. The testimonials and examples provided in this book show exceptional results, which may not apply to the average reader, and are not intended to represent or guarantee that you will achieve the same or similar results.

The Healing Paws Method

THOMAS ACOSTA

Reflexology is like pushing a button on an elevator.
When you press it, the elevator gets you to your desired floor.

Table of Contents

The power of a healing touch cannot be overestimated.

Pepe

Portrait by Elizabeth Silk

Dedication

I dedicate this book to my life partner and wife, Joey Best. Without her experienced guidance, patience, invaluable inspiration and her indomitable will to keep going when the going got tough, this book would have never tasted ink. Last but not least, I also dedicate this book to my forever, furry best friend, Pepe, who inspired me with his unconditional love and companionship.

I'm ready for this!

Foreward

In the course of the sixteen years that I have practiced veterinary medicine, I have found that some of the most profound healing actions can be those of touch.

The loving touch of an experienced and caring veterinarian upon his or her animal patient can do wonders. The feel of an owner can spark instant gratitude from their four-legged friend. Profound healing can begin with a simple touch to a devoted and loving dog or cat by their privileged owner.

The touch of love and emotion is a powerful medicine to the soul of any creature. The strengthening of the spirit of any individual, be they human or animal, can work wonders in restoring physical health. It should not surprise us then that touch, the most ancient of all therapies, can be scientifically and skillfully applied to the support and healing of dogs and cats.

Many new alternative areas of healing have recently opened up to veterinarians. Acupuncture, chiropractic and herbal medicine have all come to the forefront in the continuing effort to deal with frustrating and debilitating disease syndromes.

Now, Thomas Acosta brings us a new avenue to pursue. The *Healing Paws Method* describes a genuinely hands-on and noninvasive approach to dog and cat holistic support and treatment through the simple and basic act of touch and massage.

As the veterinary community expands its boundaries to include diagnostic and treatment modalities of varied sources and philosophies, the *Healing Paws Method* will become a valued addition to our libraries. The art of Reflexology will become an essential part of our therapeutic considerations.

Joe D. Hendricks, DVM

An experienced and loving touch by you can do wonders for their health.

Acknowledgment

I want to extend a special thank you to Dr. Joe D. Hendricks, DVM, for his help and guidance in creating this book. I am grateful that as a medical professional, he believes in the notion that healing can take many forms and that alternatives to conventional medicine are always on the table.

I also would like to acknowledge the work of Thomas J. Jenkins in his book *Functional Mammalian Neuroanotomy* and the work of Dr. Pitcairn in his book *A Complete Guide to Natural Healing for Cats and Dogs.* The wisdom in those pages assisted tremendously in my understanding of the many possibilities of alternative treatments for pets.

I want to extend special thanks to my sister Ida DiFlavio and my late brother-in-law Marty DiFlavio for encouraging me to write it.

And thank you, Geri Shultz, a dog trainer and good friend, for offering a trove of information on the nature of our canine friends.

Thanks to Wendy Lippman (owner of Tlaquepaque in Sedona, Arizona) and her loyal friend Floyd for posing with Reflexology positions.

And an extra-special thank you to my talented wife, Joey Best. Without her guidance, formidable writing skills, advice and support, I would have never brought this book to its completion.

Last but not least is my forever, furry best friend, Pepe, who inspired me with his unconditional love and companionship.

It should not surprise us that touch, the most ancient of all therapies, can be scientifically and skillfully applied to the support and healing of dogs and cats.

Preface

Reflexology! A gift from the ancients! It's one of the humblest of the healing arts because the feet are where the work is applied.

Reflexology is considered one of the most effective alternative healing modalities of all for humans. Here's the good news! Reflexology is not just for people! This same tried and true method is a gift for our furry friends as well. It works and it's a simple process. All it takes is the application of gentle pressure to the paws of your dog or cat and doing it with regularity. Your animal will respond as quickly if not quicker than we humans do to Reflexology.

As you gain a deeper understanding of the anatomy and physiology of your pets, you will achieve the same for humans. Though different in our outward appearance, the inside of the bodies of humans and mammals are strikingly similar.

That is why Reflexology works just as well on them as it does on us.

Healing Paws Method is a simple guide you can use to help your pets lead happier and healthier lives. It is also an in-depth study of the physiology of animals and specific ways of applying your touch. Reflexology can be used to alleviate many ailments and pain.

Just try it because, in the end, what matters most is that you rub your pet's paws with loving intention.

You'll discover along with your pet that it's SIMPLY PAWSOME!

Reflexology Foot Chart
With Corresponding Paws

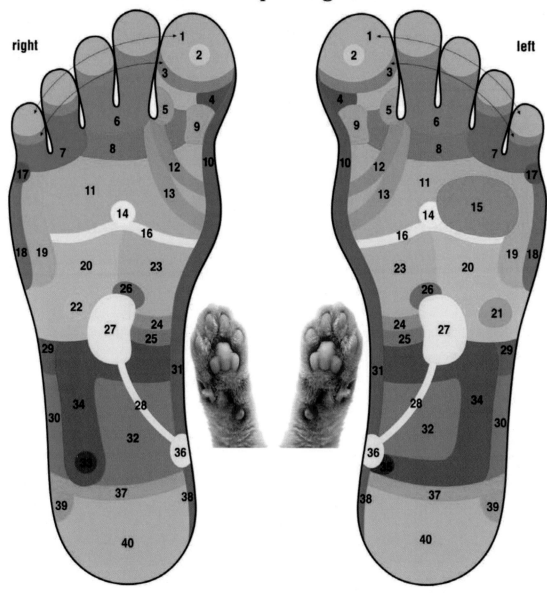

1	Head/Brain	**11**	Lung/Chest	**21**	Spleen	**31** Lumbar Vertebrae
2	Pituitary	**12**	Thyroid/Bronchia	**22**	Gall Bladder	**32** Small Intestine
3	Teeth/Sinuses	**13**	Esophagus	**23**	Stomach	**33** Appendix
4	Nose	**14**	Solar Plexus	**24**	Pancreas	**34** Colon
5	Throat	**15**	Heart	**25**	Duodenum	**35** Rectum
6	Eye	**16**	Diaphragm	**26**	Adrenals	**36** Bladder
7	Ear	**17**	Armpit	**27**	Kidney	**37** Sciatic Nerve
8	Trapezius	**18**	Arm	**28**	Ureter	**38** Knee
9	Neck	**19**	Shoulder	**29**	Elbow	**39** Sacrum
10	Cervical Spine	**20**	Liver	**30**	Hip Joint	**40** Lower Back/Gluteal Area

Introduction

What if you could address health issues with the touch of your hand?
Sounds like a snake oil cure?
Well, think again.

I have been a Reflexologist for forty years. In that time, I have seen many people helped by the incredible power of Reflexology. It is one of the most humble yet powerful modalities of the ancient healing disciplines. Paralysis, Parkinson's disease, diabetes, arthritis, liver and kidney problems, heart problems, headaches and so many other ailments I have seen respond to its almost magical touch.

Reflexology is based upon the principle that there are specific points on the feet and hands that correspond to every part of the human body. When applying pressure to those points improved health follows. As awed as I have been by seemingly miraculous recoveries through Reflexology with humans, one cannot imagine my delightful surprise upon discovering that Reflexology also works on our cherished furry-family members.

You've seen that look on your pets when they are sick or in discomfort, adorable sad eyes searching yours for help. Who would have guessed that a simple touch could give much-needed relief to your dog or cat? So little had been written on the animal connection that I had glossed over this concept and had focused only on the ailments of people. That was until I treated my first "non-human" client!

The experience left me in absolute awe of the power of Reflexology and the fact that it can be applied to pets as effectively as humans. My pet clients responded so quickly to the treatment that it almost seemed impossible. But yet, the proof was right there in front of me. It works on pets and the positive effects just can't be denied.

So read on and learn how you too can apply this simple healing technique on your pets. The power of Reflexology awaits you.

The feel of your touch can spark instant gratitude from your four-legged friend.

Chapter 1

My First Pet Client

One cannot imagine my delightful surprise upon discovering that Reflexology also works on our cherished furry-family members.

My First Pet Client

One day while visiting my sister she told me that her dog Muttly, a Terrier mix, was suffering terribly with hip pain in his right hindquarter.

Muttly was walking with great difficulty. He was standing with his right hind leg up for a moment before being able to put it down and gingerly take a few steps before stopping again. My sister asked me if I thought Reflexology would help him. I confessed I wasn't sure.

It was the Fourth of July, and Muttly was trembling with fear from the exploding fireworks outside. My sister cautioned that when he was in pain, he would not let anyone touch him. I tried approaching Muttly, but he cowered away. I asked my sister for a few pieces of cheese and called Muttly to me. He came sniffing. I was then able to lure him onto my lap. He was a relatively small dog. Muttly was still trembling even as he took the treat from my hand. I managed to get my finger on the pad of his left front paw and squeezed the center of it gently, much the same as I would apply Reflexology to a person.

In humans, the solar plexus controls stress levels and breathing patterns. The related Reflexology point is located in the center of each hand and foot. I assumed it would be the same for Muttly's paw. I think he knew that I wanted to help him. We worked out a little deal. He got the cheese as long as I got the paw. In about a minute or so, Muttly stopped shaking and his panting stopped. His eyes closed. He seemed to sleep despite the noise of the fireworks. I could tell by his deep breathing and his relaxed body that he was calm and oblivious to his surroundings. Because of the speed of his relaxation, I was confident that I had located his solar plexus reflex point. As with people, pressing the solar plexus point almost always brings about quick, deep relaxation.

In humans, the reflex point for the hip is on the outside edge of the foot midway between the toe and the heel. It is also important to note that

Profound healing can begin with a simple touch to a devoted and loving dog or cat.

the points that correspond to certain parts of the body that are out of balance are usually sensitive to touch. I figured the reflex point for Muttly's hip would be on the outside ridge of the rear paw on the same side as the problem. I surmised the point would be sensitive to my touch. I pressed it. Muttly instantly woke up and tried to pull his paw away from me. I eased the pressure and let him smell my hand that held the cheese. I continued to apply gentle pressure to that point, being careful not to

press too hard. Once again, he dozed off while I worked.

After about ten minutes of applying pressure, he awoke and started squirming. That was my signal the Reflexology session was over. I gently placed him on the ground. He took a few steps and shook himself as if to say "Hey, I'm feeling better!" A half-hour later, he was trotting around the living room. There was no doubt he was a changed dog.

He came back to me when the fireworks started going off again. I picked him up and located his solar plexus point. I stroked his head gently and pushed on the center of his left front paw. Muttly quickly calmed down and we all enjoyed the rest of the evening.

A week later, my sister called to tell me how much better Muttly was. She had continued to rub the hip reflex point on his paw as I had showed her. She was so happy. Her pet was getting along with less pain. Muttly's recovery raised the possibility that if Reflexology helps animals as well as it does humans, it would be an excellent tool for pet lovers to add to their options when tending to a sick pet or one that is in pain.

I asked my sister if she knew of any other pet owners who had tried conventional veterinary approaches and still had not found relief for their animals. She told me that she had a friend with a poodle named Jasmine. The vet had recommended that her sick dog should be put down because of the suffering it was enduring due to a badly deteriorated hip joint.

The gratitude of your loving pet when you help them is what makes it all worth it.

When I arrived at the owner's house, Jasmine was in such bad shape that the owner was carrying her outside so she could relieve herself. When Jasmine was settled, I got down on the floor next to her. I started working on the hip-reflex point. She pulled her leg away when I pressed a specific spot along the outside rim of the left-hind paw. This told me I was on the right point. It worked the same as it did with Muttly. I found the spot again and barely applied pressure. Just a light touch was enough. Before long, she was licking my hand.

During that half-hour session, I also worked the outside ridge of her left-hind paw. She stayed down and did not get up while I was there. Upon finishing, I asked the owner to call and let me know if there were any changes. When I got home I received a message. It was the happy voice of Jasmine's owner. She said that after I had left, Jasmine got up and was sniffing around happily.

I also learned that cats are a bit more challenging to work with than the dogs. One calico cat named Grouchy was not eating. I couldn't use the food trick with her because she wasn't interested. So, I had to sneak up on her while she was lying down. I managed to get hold of her paw and very gently squeeze its center. Grouchy only let me hold her a few seconds before extending a warning claw.

Taking my chances, I grabbed another paw and did the same thing. I did every paw the same way, gingerly navigating around an extended claw every so often. After a few minutes of that, she slipped my grip with an indignant meow, only to go straight to her food dish and eat!

I worked on another cat whose owner said it was hard of hearing. This cat let me rub away. She seemed to enjoy the Reflexology and purred contentedly throughout the session. I worked a spot I determined corresponded to its ears by comparing the layout of the human foot and hand to that of the animal's paw. The owner said that a few days after the treatment, the cat seemed to respond to her voice. I had shown the owner where the points for her cat's ears were so she could continue to treat her. A month later, she called to tell me that her cat was responding to her voice and other sounds.

My takeaway? Pets respond positively to Reflexology, just like humans do.

The *Healing Paws Method* was born!

This position makes it easy to work the tops and bottoms of the paws.

It is interesting to note that human and animal physiology aren't as different as you may think.

Chapter 2

Humans and Mammals Similarities

There is a biological symmetry as to the way the organs of an animal and a human are designed and placed

Humans and Mammals Similarities

An animal's nervous system is almost identical to that of a human's, as noted by Thomas W. Jenkins in his book "Functional Mammalian Neuroanatomy."

The similarity between animal and human physiology lays a foundation for the concept that Reflexology could work through an animal's nervous system as effectively and in the same manner as it does with humans. The American Veterinary Medical Association has recognized the value of Acupuncture. It works on the same principles of balancing vital life-force energy, just like Reflexology. In his book entitled the *Complete Guide to Natural Health for Dogs and Cats*, Dr. Pitcairn attests to the fact that Acupuncture can contribute to the alleviation of multiple problems. Acupuncture treatments help with musculoskeletal problems, slipped disks, arthritis, skin diseases, allergies, diarrhea, vomiting, paralysis, respiratory difficulty and a variety of illnesses that plague dogs and cats as well as humans.

Reflexology is like Acupuncture without needles. While one modality stimulates specific meridian points throughout the body with needles, Reflexology only requires gentle pressure to points on the hands or feet, where the neurological wiring from your brain ends. Either through Reflexology or Acupuncture, the results are a benefit to the host.

There is a biological symmetry as to the way the organs of an animal and a human are designed and placed. When a dog or a cat stands on their hind legs, one can see just how similar the placement of their organs is to that of ours. In descending order, the head, the neck, the lungs, the heart, the kidneys, digestive organs, eliminative organs and hips, all correspond to the human design. Reflexology affirms our biological connection

The touch of love and emotion is a powerful medicine to the soul of any creature.

to the animal world because it works on pets as well as on us. Consider the fact that our pets suffer from the same maladies we humans do and the connection becomes even more apparent.

Reflexology Is Simple

The Reflexology technique is quite straightforward. Almost anyone can apply it. As long as one is pressing the right spot for a sufficient amount of time, it works. It takes no special skills or extensive training and education. If you know the

medical condition you wish to address, and you know the point to which it corresponds, apply gentle pressure and the condition improves. Reflexology works on the same principle as Acupuncture and Acupressure. It balances the body's natural life force energy called Chi. Reflexology unblocks areas where this energy congests. A human's neurological network starts in the head and ends at the hands and feet. It's the same with our four-legged friends. The difference is their neurological systems end at their paws.

How Reflexology Works

Mammals are not only physical and spiritual manifestations. We are also "electrical" beings. It is through the body's neurological systems (the cranial nervous system, the central nervous system, the peripheral nervous system and the autonomic nervous system) that every function of our anatomy operates. When an injury or disease disrupts the flow of this biochemically-produced neurological current, the particular organ or part of the body controlled by the neurological line of transmission falls out of balance.

If this blockage of energy occurs and the energetic flow of the body's nervous system is impeded, the nerve endings at the bottoms of the hands or feet that correspond to the diseased or distressed part of the body become sensitive. The reflexologist tries to locate the points that correspond to those parts of the body. Then they gently stimulate them with finger pressure because all of the body's neurological lines of the transmission end there. This action breaks up the impedance and allows the neurological energy to flow more freely.

Always remember that in the final analysis, it is the love you share with your pet that makes the greatest difference.

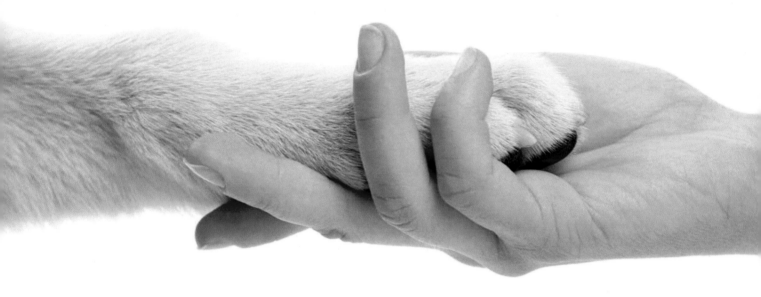

In the end, what matters most is that you rub your pet's paws with loving intention.

History of Reflexology

Reflexology has been around since at least 4000 B.C., as depicted in the tomb of Ankhmahor in Egypt. An ancient Egyptian drawing in his tomb shows a servant applying Reflexology to the feet of the king. Depictions of Reflexology in ancient times also have been found in China, the Mayan culture, Ayurvedic traditions, Indian traditions and in many other ancient cultures.

In the sixteenth century, this healing art became popular in Europe, with royalty reaping its benefits. At the turn of the nineteenth century, it was introduced to the U.S. in a book written by Eunice Ingham titled *Stories the Feet Can Tell*, printed in 1938. Since then, the healing practice has grown exponentially in popularity and has been accepted as an effective alternative healing method.

The Bottom Line

Reflexology is safe and straightforward. No one is 100 percent sure how it works. It just does. There are different theories and opinions, but the best explanation I've heard is that Reflexology is like pushing a button on an elevator. When you press it, the elevator gets you to your desired floor. Many books about Reflexology for humans have been published but not too many on Reflexology for pets. I have witnessed the incredible healing power of this holistic science with people. I have also seen animals recover their strength, health and vitality. For this reason, I wrote the *Healing Paws Method*. My dream is to share this healing gift with the pet lovers of the world. In the end, what matters most is that you rub your pet's paws with loving intention.

With this technique you can apply
pressure to the top and bottom
of the paw at the same time

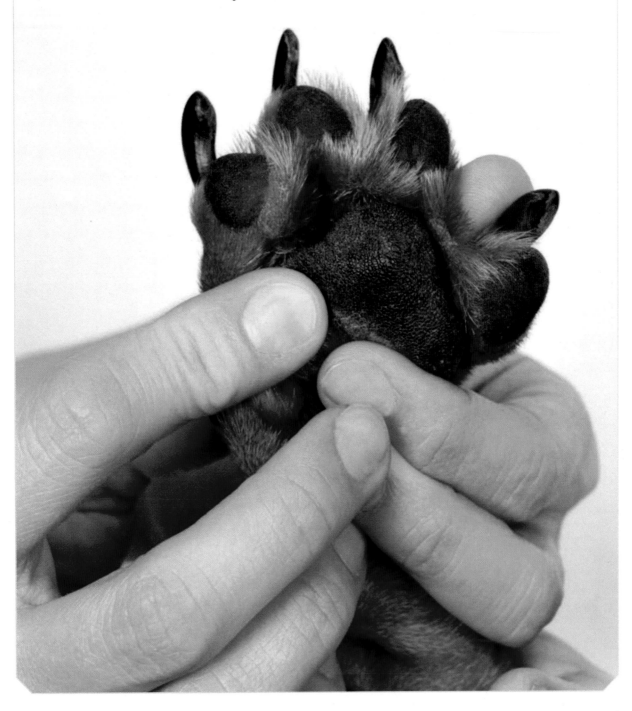

*The boundless love between a loyal pet and
its loving owner cannot be measured.*

Chapter 3

Points & Locations

What better way to share the gift of Reflexology,
than with your cherished furry friend?

Points & Locations

Reflexologists believe that the feet and hands are miniature representations of the human body and that specific points on them correspond to the body's every part.

The feet and hands act as control panels from which the entire body can be accessed. The toes represent the upper part of the body. The balls of the feet represent the chest area. The middle of the foot represents the central organs, and the heels of the foot correspond to the sex and eliminative organs. The outer edges of the feet correspond to the outside perimeter of the body, such as the arms, hips, and shoulders. The inner edges of the feet correspond to the center of the body, such as the spine and back.

If you had a headache, for instance, look for a point on your big toe, which represents the center of your head. The ear reflex is located at the base of the baby toe. For a heart problem, the point would be found in the center of the left pad of your foot. If you suffer from a lower digestive tract problem, the point would be located near the bottom of both feet.

Understanding that an animal's neurological system and anatomy are almost identical to humans, one can map the reflex points for an animal in a similar fashion as one would for a person. In an animal, the toe pads represent the points in an animal's head: the eyes, ears, brain, sinuses, teeth, tongue, etc. The central pad below the toe pads would represent the chest, lungs, heart, kidneys, pancreas, spleen, digestive organs and eliminative organs, depending on what part of the pad you were working on at the time.

The upper part of the pad would reflect the upper organs such as the lungs and heart. Going towards the middle of the pad would indicate the stomach, kidneys, adrenal glands and stomach. The lower part of the pad would correspond to the sex glands and eliminative organs. As it is for humans, so it is for dogs and cats.

See your pet regain their health and vitality with Reflexology.

Reflexology Charts

If you look at various Reflexology charts for humans, you may notice that there is always a slight variation as to the exact location of the Reflexology points. The points may not be exactly where the chart indicates but mostly in the general vicinity. Therefore, it's always best to apply what I consider the number one rule of Reflexology. If it hurts, rub it!

You can generally tell when you're on the right spot on a human by its tenderness. If the organ or gland it connects with is out of balance, that reflex point will also be sensitive. With humans, it's easier to know you are on a spot because you will get an "ouch!" With animals, it's more difficult

because they can't speak. They will, however, pull their paws away when you're on a sensitive spot. Some animals may try to bite or bark if their paws are too sensitive. Gentleness, bribes with treats and persistence are the key to getting your pet to let you work on their paws.

I created the *Healing Paws Method* charts so you can refer to them when working on your own pet. I indicate specific locations that I found to be sensitive in animals when their medical conditions were known. By following the same principles of zone therapy in human Reflexology, I was able to put together what I believe is a reasonably comprehensive map of these points on animal paws.

I found that specific areas of sensitivity corresponded to specific medical conditions. For example, animals with digestive problems were sensitive to pressure on the lower part of their pads, just as humans would be on the lower part of their feet. Animals with hearing problems were sensitive on the bottom part of their outside toe pads, just as humans would be on the bottom part of their little toe and so on.

The best way to use the *Healing Paws Method* charts is to locate the general vicinity of a particular reflex point on the paw and push gently on and around it until a sensitive spot is found. You'll know when you hit these spots with animals because they will pull their paws away or turn their head at you in a quizzical way. They might lick your hand, or their ears might perk up. One way or another, they'll let you know. The trick is not to let the animal pull entirely away. Use any technique you need to, especially bribes, with treats to keep them with you. Try to press the points as long as you can. It's best to work all four paws. But if you can't, then settle for what you can get.

On the next two pages refer to the *Healing Paws Method Charts* detailing all the Reflexology points on the paws that correspond to your pet's physiology.

Reflexology balances the body's natural life force energy called Chi. Reflexology unblocks areas where this energy congests.

REFLEXOLOGY POINTS
FOR DOGS & CATS

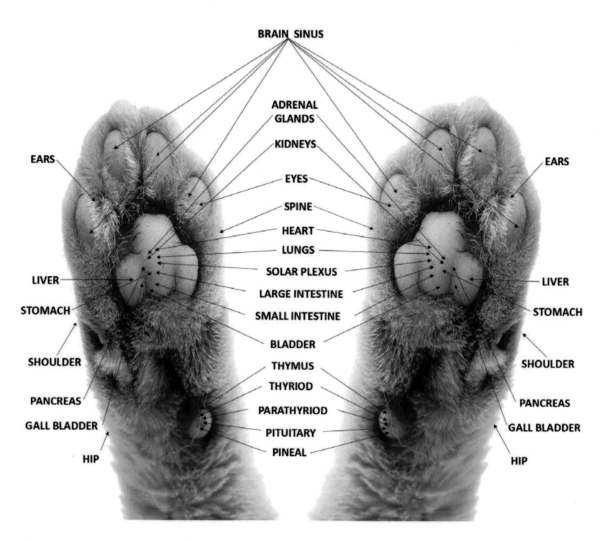

BRAIN SINUS

ADRENAL GLANDS

KIDNEYS

EARS

EYES

SPINE

HEART

LUNGS

LIVER

SOLAR PLEXUS

LARGE INTESTINE

STOMACH

SMALL INTESTINE

SHOULDER

BLADDER

THYMUS

PANCREAS

THYRIOD

GALL BLADDER

PARATHYRIOD

HIP

PITUITARY

PINEAL

EARS

LIVER

STOMACH

SHOULDER

PANCREAS

GALL BLADDER

HIP

RIGHT **LEFT**

Pleae note that given the size of most paws, when applying pressure
your finger will cover multiple Reflexology points. It's always best to move
your fingers slightly to the left or right, up and down
while applyingt pressure to make sure all the points are covered.
You can usually tell when you hit
a sensitive point because your pet will give you a clue
by pulling away, looking at you or squirming.

As with human Reflexology where it can be applied to the hands or feet,
Reflexology for pets can be applied to all four paws.

REFLEXOLOGY POINTS
FOR TOP AND SIDES OF PAWS

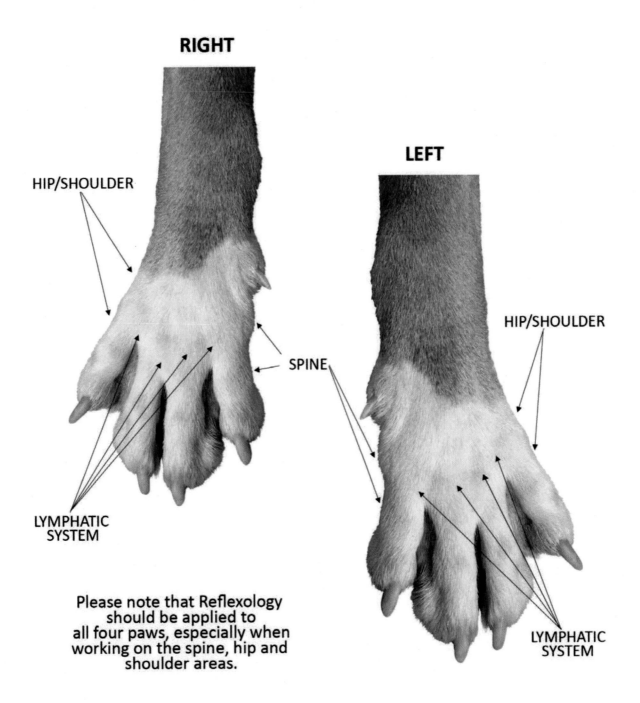

RIGHT

HIP/SHOULDER

SPINE

LYMPHATIC SYSTEM

LEFT

HIP/SHOULDER

LYMPHATIC SYSTEM

Please note that Reflexology should be applied to all four paws, especially when working on the spine, hip and shoulder areas.

The same applies when working the Lymphatic System. Work the entire top of each paw to ensure complete coverage.

*You can't imagine the satisfaction you will feel
from being able to help your best friend in distress.*

CHAPTER 4

Reflexology for Organs & Glands

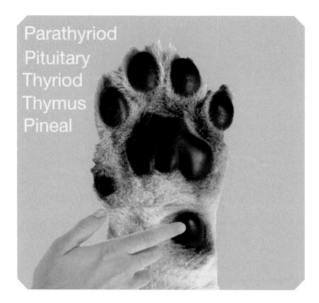

Parathyriod
Pituitary
Thyriod
Thymus
Pineal

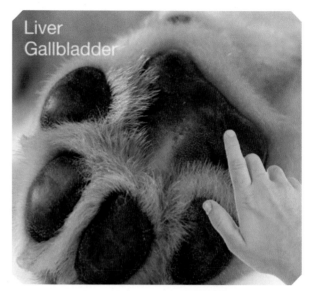

Liver
Gallbladder

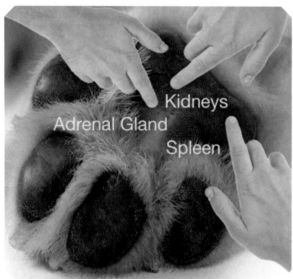

Kidneys
Adrenal Gland
Spleen

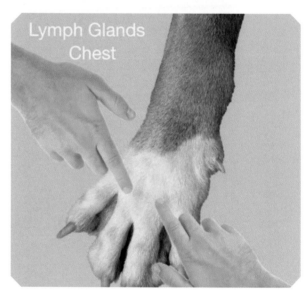

Lymph Glands
Chest

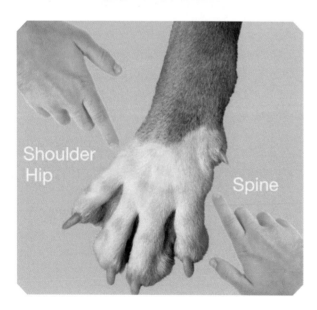

Shoulder
Hip
Spine

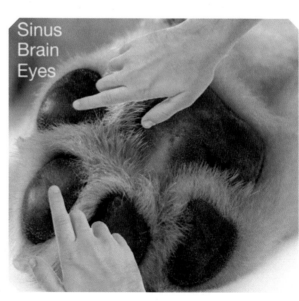

Sinus
Brain
Eyes

Reflexology for Organs & Glands

Please refer to the main charts on pages 22 and 23 to locate the specific points. Remember, the smaller the pads, the more area your thumb or forefinger will cover, meaning you will be working more than one point at a time. The following is a listing of the organs and glands you will be working on, their functions, and how to apply Reflexology to them.

BLADDER

The bladder stores urine before expelling it out of the body. When the bladder reaches a certain point of fullness, it triggers the urinary track to release its contents. Infections of the bladder can impede the flow of urine and toxins will build up in the body as a result.

In animals, the bladder is located at the bottom center of the large pad on all four paws.

A workout of this reflex point will ensure proper elimination of urine from the body and prevent infections.

BRAIN

All the functions of the body are controlled by the brain. It is the central processing center for all information and exterior stimuli. The brain determines an organism's intelligence and its ability to navigate and survive in its environment. Beginning with the dewclaw, the reflexes for the brain stretch across the tips of each of the toe pads. The dewclaw corresponds to the middle brain. Each toe pad from the inner to the outer edge corresponds to different parts of the brain. Toe pads should be worked in the same manner as the dewclaw. Thoroughly work one toe pad at a time. Start from the dewclaw and work your way through the upper toe pads.

Working the brain reflex point helps improve memory and attention span in animals.

DUODENUM, SMALL INTESTINE, AND LARGE INTESTINE

The duodenum passes food from the stomach to the small intestine where it is absorbed into the body. The small intestine then sends what is not digested to the large intestine where it is further processed and then eliminated from the body. These parts of the digestive tract can be reflexed on all four large pads. Begin at the bottom of the pads and work your way across the entire pad. Any problems dealing with poor elimination or absorption of food can be addressed at these points.

A workout of these reflexes keeps your pet's digestive and eliminative organs operating at peak performance. It helps to soothe indigestion and upset stomachs as well as fight constipation.

EYES AND EARS

The outer toe pads are the stimulus points for the eyes and ears. The paws on the right side hold the reflex points for the right eye and ear. Points on the left side correspond to the left eye and ear. These points are very close together, so you will most likely be working the eye and ear reflexes at

the same time. You will find these points low on the toe pad near the base of the main pad where they meet.

Also, work the ridge of the outer toe pad. During a full session, start from the top of the toe pads and work your way down to the bottom of the paw. Make sure you are covering both the top and bottom. Make sure to hit every Reflexology point. You can always work specific problems by locating the point on the charts and concentrating your energy there.

A workout of the ear reflexes helps clear ear infections and improves hearing. Working the eye reflexes improves vision, helps to prevent cataracts and other eye disorders and staves off blindness by improving blood circulation to the eyes.

Did I hear that right?

Working the digestive system
with your thumb

Working the Dewclaw with your thumb

GALL BLADDER

The gall bladder sits under the liver, storing bile, which is necessary for the digestion of fats and the absorption of such fat-soluble vitamins as A, D and K. Bile also encourages food to move along the digestive tract. The reflex point for the gall bladder is on the large pads of the animal's right paws, on the inner, middle part of the pad.

A workout of this reflex helps to improve vision, promote healthy bones, fight tooth decay, prevent gallstones and control cholesterol levels.

HEART

The heart reflex for animals can be discovered in the center of the large pad. No muscle in the body works harder than the heart, which beats millions of times throughout a lifetime and pumps hundreds of thousands of gallons of blood throughout the body. Any heart problem can be addressed at this point, including high blood pressure and weakness in any of its valves.

A good workout of the heart reflex will do wonders to improve adverse conditions and increase circulation, stamina, endurance and strength. Animals, like humans, are affected by stress, and the heart can take a beating when tension prevails in an organism's existence. Be sure that your animal knows it is loved and that it has exercise and space.

KIDNEYS

The kidneys filter waste and toxins from the blood. They pass the debris out of the body in the form of urine. Kidneys are invaluable to the body, and without them, one would die in a matter of hours. The reflex point for the kidneys can be found on the large pads on all four paws.

The pads on the animal's left side will correspond to the left kidney and the pads on the right side to the right kidney. The point will be low on the outside center of the large pad. Pets who don't drink enough freshwater often develop kidney problems.

A good workout of these reflex points will help keep their kidneys healthy and eliminate toxic buildup. When the kidneys can't eliminate toxins, the liver has to work extra hard to do its job.

LIVER

The liver is the body's chemical factory, producing dozens of vital chemicals necessary to maintain life and health. It filters toxic waste products and stores vitamins and minerals, including iron, which is needed to produce red blood cells. It also produces antibodies and blood clotting compounds as well as bile.

There are over a thousand physical problems associated with the liver. A workout of this organ is vital. In both dogs and cats, the liver reflex is located along the middle meridian of the large pad of the right-side paws. The liver is a large organ and part of it stretches into the left paw pad as well. While working the liver reflex, you will also be working the gall bladder, which stores bile and releases it into the stomach when needed.

Work outward from the inner and middle sections of the pad. Try to spend at least five minutes on this point. Be careful though not to exceed that time, especially in animals that are highly toxic or have terrible diets. Reflexology can spark a healing crisis and the animal may develop loose bowels.

A workout of the liver stimulates the organ to strengthen the body's immune system, neutralize poisons and dispose of bacteria and other foreign matter. It will help the liver to perform its many functions and will help keep the whole body in good working order.

LUNGS

It is through the lungs that the blood gets its oxygen to maintain life. Lung problems can significantly reduce an animal's quality of life. The reflex points for the lungs lie in the center of the main pad. If you rub the entire pad, the lungs will be completely addressed. Begin where the main pad meets the toe pads from the inside of the paw. Work your way down towards the bottom of the pad. This action will help open the bronchial tubes, loosen tightened chest muscles and strengthen the diaphragm, which is the muscle that pumps the lungs.

Working the lung reflexes will help increase your dog's wind and stamina. Work this point for any kind of breathing disorder.

LYMPHATIC SYSTEM

The lymphatic system is basically the body's carwash, as well as the foundation of its immune defense mechanism. Lymph fluid, which is in the lymph glands and vessels, carries away dead cells and debris from the body's organs. Lymph fluid contains lymphocytes, the cells that kill invading organisms and fight disease and infection.

The reflex points for the lymphatic system for animals lie along the top of the paws. Apply pressure along the top of the paw upwards toward the animal's anklebone. Don't press too hard and maintain a steady rhythm and rub in little circles. This part can be sensitive. By pressing these points on all four paws, you can be confident you are covering the entire system.

A good reflexology workout of the lymph gland reflexes helps an animal to live longer, feel more energetic, resist disease better and maintain a healthy shining coat.

PANCREAS

The pancreas regulates the sugar levels of the body. When the pancreas is out of balance, diabetes begins. This reflex point is more towards the middle of the left paw and stretches across to the right paw.

By working these points, you help maintain a healthy pancreas and balanced levels of insulin. Dogs that lose energy during the day for no apparent reason may be suffering from pancreatic misbalance. Reflexology can help bring them back.

PITUITARY GLAND

The pituitary gland is the body's commander-in-chief of the endocrine system. The pituitary gland controls the functions of all the other organs through the secretions of certain chemicals called hormones. Located in the center of the brain is the pituitary gland. In humans, the reflex point can be found in the center of the big toe or thumb.

In animals, there is a fifth toe pad, which is higher up along the leg than the other four. The pituitary gland reflex point is located on the inside ridge of the fifth toe pad. It is called the dewclaw. It is tiny in comparison to the other toe pads. The dewclaw is the equivalent of the big toe or thumb for a human. This point is so small that it can be squeezed between the thumb and forefinger and be covered entirely. Press it. Hold it for at least ten seconds or as long as you can. Release and repeat.

Depending on how long your pet will sit for a session, you can increase or decrease the duration of the pressure and the number of your repetitions. The more impatient they are, the less time you have. Bribes work well in such situations. Pressing this point will stimulate the pituitary gland to release the hormones the other organs need to function correctly.

This reflex point helps with problems of the liver, spleen, adrenal glands, sex glands, thyroid and parathyroid glands. It helps puppies and kittens grow bigger and stronger. As a bonus, it can also help them sleep better. After the solar plexus, this should be the next point to work.

REPRODUCTIVE ORGANS

The sex organ points are located at the inner bottom of the pads. These points include the lower corners of all four paws and the dewclaw. To work these reflex points, pinch the bottom part of the dewclaw between your thumb and first finger and then hold. Also, the outer edges of the bottom parts of the paws should be worked.

Working these points maintains hormonal balance and ensures proper sexual development, especially for breeding. These points are also essential to work on in animals that have been neutered.

Reflexology will put in your hands the power to transform your love into a healing tool.

SINUSES

The reflexes for an animal's sinuses and snout are also in the toe pads, just a little lower down than the reflex points for the brain. Your thumb or forefinger will cover both the brain and sinus points at the same time. Tenderness in these points could indicate a misbalance in either area.

A workout of these points will help your pet breath easier and keep their nasal passages healthy.

SOLAR PLEXUS

The solar plexus is a bundle of nerves in the center of the body, which controls the muscles and organs in the abdominal area. It behaves like a body's second brain for transmitting fear or peace, depending on what the physical and emotional conditions are.

When there is fear, the solar plexus commands the adrenal glands to release adrenaline, putting the body into a fight or flight mode. When all is calm, the solar plexus sends messages to the stomach and the digestive organs that all is well and to perform their functions smoothly and without stress.

The solar plexus point for pets is located in the center of the middle pad on all four paws. Work all the paws when conducting a full session. The best technique to follow and assure maximum coverage is to thoroughly work each paw, one at a time, before going on to the next.

Press the point for the solar plexus and hold it for a few seconds. You can use any finger you like. If the dog is lying with its stomach on your lap, then it's easier to press with your forefinger or index finger. If it's on its back with its legs facing up at you, then it's easier to press with your thumb. There are many different approaches. Adjust to the one where you and your animal feel the most comfortable. Don't press too hard. Apply smooth and gentle but steady pressure to the point.

A good workout of the solar plexus point helps alleviate nervousness, irritability, stomach problems, allergies and heavy breathing. You should hold this point until the animal starts to relax. Just be patient and persistent.

SPLEEN

The spleen is situated to the left of the stomach on the left side of the animal's body. The spleen cleanses and recycles red blood cells, filters lymph fluid and produces lymphocytes (disease-fighting cells). The reflex point for the spleen can be found three-quarters of the way down the large pad along its outer edge. Work the pancreas reflex point and you will be addressing the spleen as well.

A workout of this point will increase the body's resistance to disease and increase strength and energy as it helps to nourish red blood cells. Anemic conditions will improve with regular workouts of the spleen reflex.

Lucky Floyd enjoys a Reflexology work out from his loving mom, Wendy.
Now that's one happy Golden Retriever.

 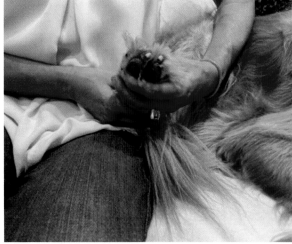

Wendy demonstrates various positions for your Reflexology session.

STOMACH

The stomach is situated mostly on the left side. It stretches across the body in dogs and cats into the right side as well. Therefore, you will work from the inner part of the large left pad inward, slightly below the centerline of the pad.

The stomach is the principal organ of digestion. It can be subject to numerous problems, including gas, indigestion, ulcers, nausea, bloating, and toxic gastritis, which can result from swallowing poisons. Also, hydrochloric acid can burn a hole through the stomach lining when extreme stressful conditions are experienced.

Give this point a good workout to increase appetite, improve digestion and alleviate gas pains or the pain of an upset stomach.

THYMUS AND PINEAL GLANDS

The thymus gland produces disease-fighting cells. The pineal gland regulates sleep patterns and moods. The reflex for the pineal gland can be found in the same area as the pituitary. The thymus reflex is located under the first toe pad.

Working these points will help improve your pet's immune system and sleep better.

THYROID GLAND AND PARATHYROID

The thyroid gland controls the metabolic functions of the body. The parathyroid glands control the loss of calcium from an organism's bones. Situated on the inner edge of the dewclaw is the reflex point to the parathyroid glands. The thyroid gland reflex is located on the dewclaw. Work up and down the inner ridge.

A workout of the thyroid and parathyroid glands will help keep your dog's metabolism in balance, keep it calm, and maintain strong bones into old age. Sometimes hyperactivity in an animal can be traced to a misbalance in the thyroid gland. The same is also true for sluggishness.

Reflexology enhances the bond between you and your pet.

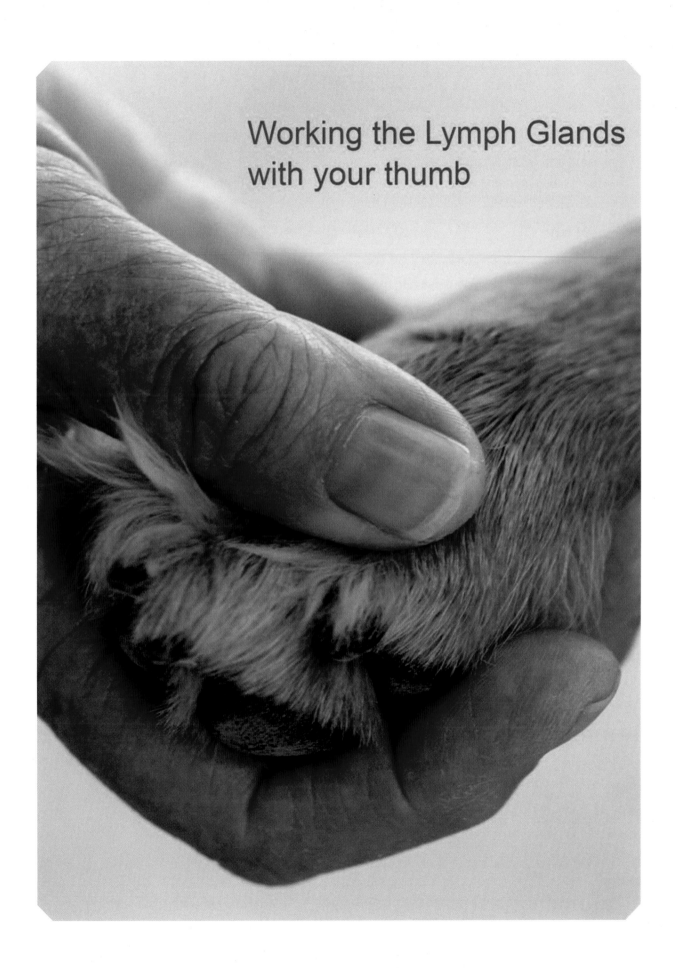

Working the Lymph Glands
with your thumb

Basic Reflexology Workout Tips

Reflexology is one of the best holistic preventive measures out there to keep the body healthy, resilient and resistant to disease. A good workout of the entire physiological system in humans and pets does wonders for keeping everything in the body functioning like a well-tuned sports car. A thorough workout means applying touch or pressure to every point on your animal's paws, during one session and on a regular basis to keep them going strong, even into their later years.

When administering a comprehensive session there are a couple of things to keep in mind. Depending on the size of your pet and its paws, locating the points might be somewhat difficult on a smaller one and easier to isolate on a larger dog's paw. For a smaller pet, you can actually address multiple points at one time with the tip of your finger. As long as you are able to cover all the points on each of the four paws, it will benefit your pet greatly.

Always remember you do not have to push or squeeze the paw pads hard to be effective. Gentle is the key word here. Even just holding a spot for a minute or so can work wonders. A good visual image is to imagine that you are finger painting and your job is to "paint" each of the Reflexology points on your pet's paws.

You can apply pressure with your thumb or your fingers depending on your angle of approach. You can press and hold a point or move your finger in a circular pattern. What's most important is that you give each spot you are pushing at least 30 seconds of time before moving on to another.

It's best to begin with the solar plexus reflex point to get your pet into a relaxed state. You can place your pet across your lap and work that point with your finger. Sit on the floor with your pet and work the point with your finger or you can roll your pet on its back and work that point with your thumb. Just find the approach that works best for you and your pet. Don't forget about bribing them with treats.

After the solar plexus you can work the dewclaw by squeezing it between your thumb and forefinger for a few minutes and from there move to the toe pads and cover them all with your touch. Thirty seconds each will suffice. Next, go for the center toe pad and cover it with your touch. Just gently press it and let your fingers cover it entirely as if you were painting it with energy.

Do the same for all four paws if you can. Linger and stay on any point that appears to be sensitive to your animal. Sensitivity in Reflexology generally means there could be a disbalance in that particular gland or organ that spot refers to. Always give these spots extra time.

The power of a loving touch cannot be overestimated. Share the love #healingpawsmethod on Instagram.

CHAPTER 5

Top Ailments Affecting Dogs

The power of Reflexology awaits you.

Top Ailments Affecting Dogs

Specific Treatment Plans for Specific Ailments

The following is a list given to me by Dr. Joe Hendricks,
naming the top ailments that most commonly affect dogs.
I have put together a comprehensive *Healing Paws Method* treatment plan
for each of these specific ailments. Just follow the suggestions, charts and directions.
The particular points are highlighted on the corresponding chart
and the reason for working these points is also stated.

COLITIS SYMPTOMS

Colitis is an inflammation of the mucous membrane that lines the colon. Colitis is characterized by pain in the abdomen, with alternating episodes of constipation and diarrhea. The presence of mucus or of mucus tinged with blood in the stools shows the predominance of colitis. It can be very painful.

TREATMENT

Start by working on the solar plexus reflex. This will help to relax abdominal muscles. Next, press the adrenal gland reflex point to assist the body to secrete norepinephrine. The adrenal gland helps to maintain intestinal muscle tone by producing hydrocortisone to reduce tissue inflammation. Then work the large and small intestine reflex points to increase blood circulation and life force energy. Complete the therapy by rubbing the lymph reflexes to mobilize a strong response to infection.

COLITIS

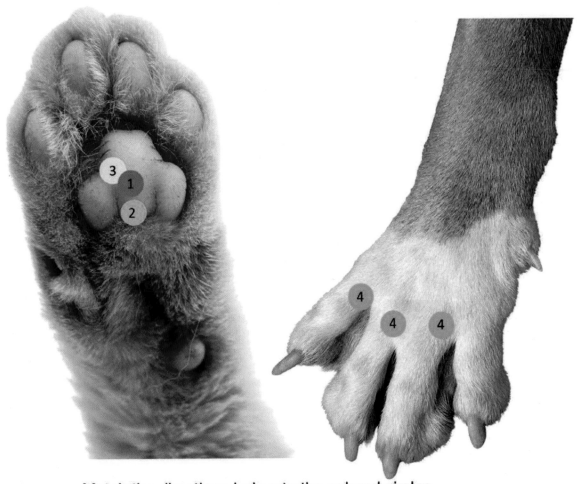

Match the directions below to the colored circles above to locate the specific points.

1 Work the solar plxus reflex point to relax the abdominal muscles.

2 Work the large and small intestine reflex point to increse life-force energy.

3 Work the adrenal gland reflex to secrete norepinephrine and hydrocortisone.

4 Work on the lymphatic system to remove dead cells and bacteria.

DIABETES SYMPTOMS

Diabetes is a disease in which the body's ability to produce or respond to the hormone insulin is impaired, resulting in abnormal metabolism of carbohydrates and elevated levels of glucose in the blood and urine. Symptoms often include frequent urination, increased thirst and increased appetite.

TREATMENT

You need to begin treatment by working the pancreas reflex to bring your pet's system into balance. Start by pressing the pituitary reflex to stimulate the other glands. Next, massage the adrenal gland to aid in the metabolism of starches. Lastly, press the spleen, thyroid, thymus, and parathyroid reflexes to strengthen the entire endocrine system.

DIABETES

Match the directions below to the colored circles above to locate the specific points.

1. Work the adrenal gland to aid in the metabolism of starches.

2. Work the pituitary gland reflex point to stimulate the other glands.

3. Work the pancreas reflex point to stimulate it and bring it into balance.

4. Work on the spleen reflex point to filter the lymphatic system.

5. Work the thyriod, thymus and parathyriod reflex points to strenghten the entire endocrine system.

EPILEPSY SYMPTOMS

Epilepsy is a neurological disorder marked by sudden recurrent episodes of sensory disturbance, loss of consciousness, or convulsions, associated with abnormal electrical activity in the brain. Epileptic attacks are sometimes accompanied by loss of consciousness and control of bowel or bladder function.

TREATMENT

Begin by working the reflexes to the brain and the pituitary gland to increase blood circulation and neurological function. Follow by addressing the solar plexus to relax muscle tension. Proceed to the adrenal reflexes to regulate water and mineral levels in the body and reduce inflammation. Next, press the pineal gland reflexes to stimulate the production of melatonin, which has a calming effect on the animal. Continue to the thyroid reflexes to regulate metabolism. Finish by massaging the solar plexus to encourage steady and deep breathing.

EPILEPSY

Match the directions below to the colored circles above to locate the specific points.

1   Work the brain and the pituitary gland to increase blood circulation and neurological function.

2   Work the solar plexus point to relax muscle tension.

3   Work the adrenal gland reflex point to help reduce inflamation through the release of hydrocortisone.

4   Work on the pineal gland point to stimulate the production of melatonin.

5   Work the thyroid gland to regulate the metabolism.

HAY FEVER & ALLERGIC SKIN DISEASES SYMPTOMS

Hay fever is an allergic condition affecting the mucous membranes of the upper respiratory tract and the eyes, most often characterized by nasal discharge, sneezing and itchy, watery eyes. An allergic skin reaction occurs when the body attacks a foreign substance that typically does not pose a threat.

TREATMENT

All types of skin reactions and allergies are addressed at the adrenal gland reflexology points, where they regulate the metabolism of fats, proteins and carbohydrates. They also fight the inflammation of sebaceous glands and ducts. Begin by working the kidney reflexes to filter out toxic substances and regulate water balance in the tissues. Move onto the liver reflex to release Vitamin A for balanced skin oils and to release antibodies to fight infection. Concentrate also on the pituitary gland reflex points to balance the other glands. Conclude with the lymphatic reflex points to remove wastes and to release antibodies to fight skin infections.

HAYFEVER AND ALLERGIC SKIN DISEASES

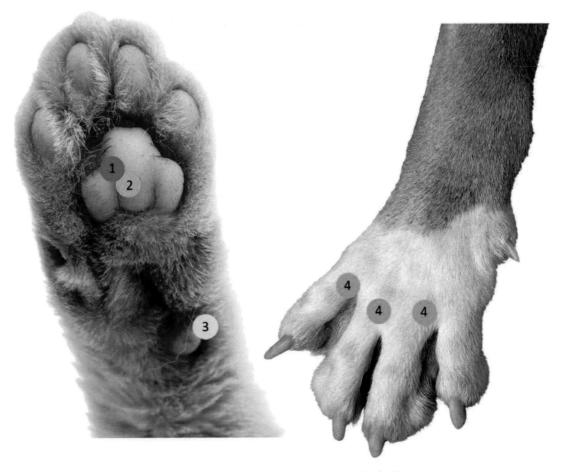

Match the directions below to the colored circles above to locate the specific points.

1. Work the liver reflex points to release Vitamin A for balanced skin oils and to release antibiotics to fight infection.

2. Work the kidney reflex points to filter out toxic substances.

3. Work on the pituitary gland reflex points to balance the other glands.

4. Work on the lymphatic reflex points to remove wastes and to release antibodies to fight skin infections.

HEART FAILURE SYMPTOMS

Heart failure is a chronic, progressive condition in which the heart muscle is unable to pump enough blood to meet the body's needs for blood and oxygen. Basically, the heart can't keep up and is unable to provide adequate blood flow to other organs such as the brain, liver and kidneys.

TREATMENT

Work the reflex points to the heart to increase blood circulation, strengthen the heart muscle and decrease pressure in the chest. Work the solar plexus and diaphragm reflex points to relax the chest muscles and to encourage relaxation and deep breathing. Work the lung reflexes to oxygenate the blood better. Work the pituitary gland to increase blood circulation and to improve glandular function. Spend a lot of time on the heart reflex and solar plexus points.

HEART FAILURE

Match the directions below to the colored circles
above to locate the specific points.

1 Work the heart reflex point to increase blood circulation.
   strenghten the heart muscle and decrease chest pressure.

2 Work the solar plexus point to to relax the chest muscles.

3 Work the lung reflex points to oxyginate the the blood better.

4 Work the diaphram reflex point to encourage relaxation
   and deep breathing.

5 Work the pituitary gland to increase blood circulation and
   improve glandular function.

HIP & SPINAL ARTHRITIS SYMPTOMS

Arthritis is the swelling and tenderness of one or more joints. The main symptoms are joint pain and stiffness, which typically worsen with age. The most common types of arthritis are osteoarthritis and rheumatoid arthritis. Arthritis and in dogs and cats affects the hip and spine, causing significant pain.

TREATMENT

Work the solar plexus reflex to relax the body. Addressing the hip and spine reflexes will increase blood circulation and enhance the flexibility of the spinal cord. Use the kidney reflexes to stimulate the kidneys to remove fluid wastes, which collect around joints. Massaging the adrenal reflexes will release hydro-cortisone to reduce inflammation. The thyroid and parathyroid gland reflex points should be worked to regulate muscle tension. Press the hip reflexes on all four paws located on the lower, outer ridge of each to achieve this.

Owners of large dogs that run a lot should regularly work the outer edges of their animal's paws. This method will keep the life-force energy flowing in their hips. A gentle and rolling massage after a run will also help slow the deterioration process.

HIP AND SPINAL ARTHRITIS

Match the directions below to the colored circles above to locate the specific points.

1. Work the solar plexus to relax the body.

2. Work the kidney reflex points to remove fluids that accumulate around the joints.

3. Work the adrenal gland reflex point to help reduce inflamation through the release of hydrocortisone.

4. Work on the hip and spine reflex points to increase blood circulation and enhance flexibility of the spinal cord.

5. Work the thyriod and parathyroid gland reflex points to regulate and ease muscle tension.

KIDNEY FAILURE SYMPTOMS

Kidney failure is the inability of the kidneys to excrete wastes and maintain the electrolyte balance. It is also known as renal failure that is the loss of the kidney's ability to function normally. Kidney failure can be fatal if left untreated. Healthy kidneys are vital to life.

TREATMENT

Vigorously work the reflexes to the kidneys to bring them back into balance. Spend a lot of time on these points. Massage the adrenal glands to regulate the mineral and water levels in the body. Also, press the pituitary gland to send chemical messages to the other organs to perform their respective tasks properly. Treat the spleen to filter the lymphatic system. Finally, press the lymph reflexes to stimulate the removal of debris from the body and work the bladder reflex to eliminate urine.

KIDNEY FAILURE

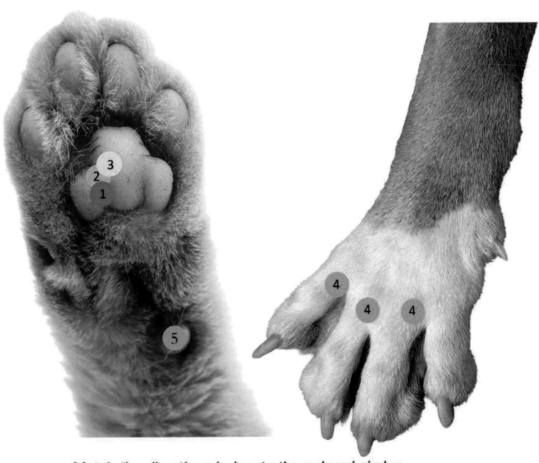

Match the directions below to the colored circles above to locate the specific points.

1 Work the bladder reflex to eliminate urine.

2 Work the kidney reflex points help them flush themselves and bring them back into balance.

3 Work the adrenal gland reflex point to regulate the mineral and water levels.

4 Work on the lymphatic system to stimulate removal of debris from the body.

5 Work the pituitary gland reflex point to send chemical messages to the other glands to perform optimally.

LIVER DISEASE SYMPTOMS

Liver disease is any disturbance of liver function that causes illness. The liver is responsible for many critical functions within the body and should it become diseased or injured, the loss of those functions can cause significant damage to the body. Liver disease is also referred to as hepatic disease. Symptoms include loss of appetite, yellowish eyes or tongue, weakness, blood in urine or stool, loss of appetite and weight loss.

TREATMENT

Work the pituitary and liver reflexes to help the liver regenerate. Next, press the spleen reflex to produce healthy red blood cells. Continue by massaging the thyroid reflex to regulate metabolism. Finally, work the lymph gland reflexes to stimulate the thymus to produce disease-fighting cells.

LIVER DISEASE

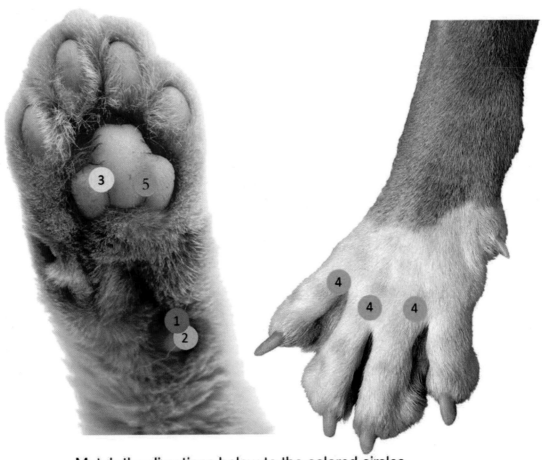

Match the directions below to the colored circles above to locate the specific points.

1   Work the thyroid gland reflex to regulate metabolism.

2   Work the pituitary reflex points help the liver regenrate.

3   Work the liver reflex point to help bring it back into balance.

4   Work on the lymphatic system to stimulate the thymus gland to produce disease fighting cells.

5   Work the spleen reflex to produce healthy red blood cells..

PANCREATITIS SYMPTOMS

Pancreatitis is an inflammation of the pancreas, an organ that is important in digestion. Pancreatitis is inflammation of the pancreas. It happens when digestive enzymes start digesting the pancreas itself. Pancreatitis can be acute or chronic. Either form is serious and can lead to complications. Acute pancreatitis occurs suddenly and usually goes away in a few days with treatment. Symptoms include a hunched back, repeated vomiting, diarrhea, dehydration, lethargy and fever.

TREATMENT

Work the pituitary reflex to send chemical messages to the pancreas to perform its functions. Massage the solar plexus to reduce stress and the adrenal glands to reduce inflammation. Work the liver point to produce antibodies, the pancreas reflex to improve blood circulation, the lymph reflexes to carry away debris and produce lymphocytes, and the spleen reflex to filter the lymphatic system.

PANCREATITIS

Match the directions below to the colored circles above to locate the specific points.

1 Work the pancreas reflex to improve blood circulation and increase vitality.

2 Work the spleen reflex point to filter the lymphatic system.

3 Work the adrenal gland reflex point to help reduce inflamation through the release of hydrocortisone.

4 Work on the liver reflex to produce antibodies.

5 Work the pituetary reflex point to send chemical messages to the pancreas to perform its functions.

URINARY BLADDER INFECTION SYMPTOMS

A urinary bladder infection is an illness caused by bacteria. Bladder infections are the most common type of urinary tract infection and can develop in any part of the urinary tract, including the urethra, bladder, ureters, or kidneys. A bladder infection can become serious if the infection spreads to the kidneys. Symptoms include excessive licking of genitals, increased thirst, loss of appetite, frequent urination, urination in the house, bloody urine, lethargy and painful urination.

TREATMENT

There are three points involved in urinary bladder infections. They are the kidney, bladder and lymphatic reflex points. Reflexology will stimulate the kidneys to flush themselves and the bladder to lose its inflammation. Begin by working the lymphatic system. This action will help to remove dead cells and bacteria. It will also increase lymphocyte production to aid in fighting the infection. Next, work the adrenal glands to help reduce inflammation through the release of hydrocortisone. End your session by massaging the spleen reflex to produce lymphocytes and to aid in the removal of wastes from the lymph fluid.

URINARY BLADDER INFECTION

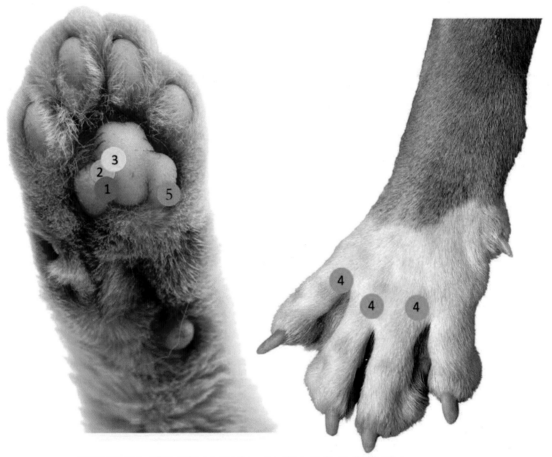

Match the directions below to the colored circles above to locate the specific points.

1 Work the bladder reflex to reduce inflammation.

2 Work the kidney reflex points help them flush themselves.

3 Work the adrenal gland reflex point to help reduce inflammation through the release of hydrocortisone.

4 Work on the lymphatic system to remove dead cells and bacteria.

5 Work the spleen reflex point to produce lymphocites and removes wastes from the lymph fluid.

I have witnessed the incredible healing power of this holistic science with people. I have also seen animals recover their strength, health and vitality.

CHAPTER 6

Top Ailments Affecting Cats

*The strengthening of the spirit of any individual, be they human or animal,
can work wonders in restoring physical health.*

Top Ailments Affecting Cats

The following are the top diseases affecting cats
and their Reflexology treatment plans.

Refer to the charts on Pages 22 & 23 for specific point locations.

CAT FIGHT ABSCESSES

Immediately work the adrenal reflexes to stimulate the production of hydrocortisone to reduce inflammation. Press the thymus, spleen and liver reflexes to launch a robust immune response to infection. Direct your pressure to the lymphatic reflexes to carry away debris and produce lymphocytes. Finish by touching the solar plexus reflexes to promote relaxation and healing.

FATTY LIVER SYNDROME

Begin by working the liver reflex to initiate healing and regeneration. Next, press the adrenal reflex to assist in the metabolism of fats. Move on to the kidney reflex points to remove toxins from the blood. Follow the lymph reflexes to cleanse tissues. Then proceed to the spleen reflex to regenerate red blood cells and filter lymph fluid. Go to the pituitary reflex to stimulate other glands to perform optimally. Complete the session by massaging the thyroid reflex to regulate metabolism.

FELINE INFECTIOUS PERITONITIS

Activate the adrenal gland reflex points to produce hydrocortisone to reduce inflammation. Next, press the liver reflex points to produce antibodies. Continue to the lymphatic reflex points to produce lymphocytes and carry away dead cells and bacteria. The next step is to address the pituitary reflex to stimulate the other glands. Move to the spleen reflex to produce healthy red blood cells and filter the lymph system. Finish by pressing the kidney reflexes to purify the blood.

LEUKEMIA VIRUS INFECTION

Begin by working the lymphatic system reflexes to stimulate the production of lymphocytes and the removal of wastes from the tissues. Also, press the spleen reflex to strengthen blood cells and filter the lymph system. Then address the pituitary gland to revitalize the other organs and the thymus reflex to produce disease-fighting cells. Next, stimulate the lung reflexes to oxygenate the blood. Finally, activate the liver reflexes to stimulate the production of antibodies.

LYMPH SARCOMA

Press the pituitary reflex to stimulate other glands to perform optimally. Then work the lymphatic system to drain itself and produce lymphocytes. Switch to the thymus reflex to produce disease-fighting cells. Massage the spleen reflex to filter the lymph system. End the treatment by pressing the solar plexus reflex points to relax the body and promote healing.

OTHER PROBLEMS FOR CATS

The *Healing Paws Method* allows you to utilize the same reflex points on cats that you use for dogs. Refer to the specific top ailment charts for dogs starting on page 41, for cats suffering from the same maladies.

Always remember that in the final analysis, it is the love you share with your pet that makes the greatest difference.

HEALTH BENEFITS OF CBD OIL

TOP 10 REASONS
TO GIVE YOUR PET CBD

HELP WITH EPILEPSY

HELP JOINS

FIGHT ARTHRITIS

STIMULATES APPETITE

IS SAVE & EFFECTIVE

REDUCE ANXIETY

FIGHT CANCER

RELIEVE PAIN

REDUCE INFLAMMATION

HELP NERVOUS SYSTEM

CHAPTER 7

CBD & Your Pet

It seems almost everyone in the world is talking about the healing properties of cannabidiol, commonly known as CBD. It is a non-psychoactive derivative from the hemp cannabis plants known to help alleviate numerous medical conditions. If your dog suffers from anxiety, epilepsy, pain, noise phobias, loss of appetite, inflammation or seizures, it is quite possible CBD oil can help alleviate those symptoms.

CBD oil has been scientifically tested and proven that it helps alleviate those same conditions in humans, which leads us to believe it works just as well in pets. According to an article published by FORBES in 2018 titled *Cornell University Research Could Help Hemp Entrepreneurs–And Make Dogs Feel Better*, author Julia Weed makes a case for the efficacy of CBD in treating pain associated with osteoarthritis in dogs. She cites a study conducted by Dr. Joe Wakshlag of Cornell University's College of Veterinary Medicine, who tested CBD oil to see if it could help dogs who are experiencing pain

from osteoarthritis. His results were published in *Frontiers in Veterinary Science* in July of 2018.

According to the author, this was a double-blind placebo trial studying dogs that were suffering from osteoarthritis and multi-joint pain. The results were significant, according to the researchers, with over 80 percent of the dogs taking the CBD oil showing significant improvement in pain levels and quality of life, without discernible side effects. There have been numerous tests and scientific studies conducted to date. Additional benefits of CBD oil for dogs can be found by simply researching findings on the Internet. One can also find companies that sell CBD products.

As science continues to improve and redefine the benefits of CBD there will be many more outlets to choose from providing this wonderful new healing product for our pets. CBD can be a beneficial addition to your pet's Reflexology regimen when addressing physical ailments like pain, anxiety and many others.

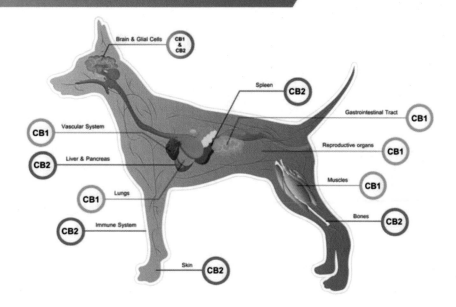

YOUR CATS CANNABINOID RECEPTORS

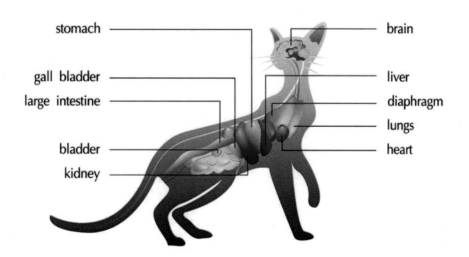

stomach — brain

gall bladder — liver

large intestine — diaphragm

— lungs

bladder — heart

kidney

CB1 & CB2

Gall Bladder
Brain Stem
Bone Marrow
Liver
Pancreas

CB1

Brain
Gastrointestinal tract
Lungs
Muscles
Reproductive Organs
Vascular System

CB2

Bones
Brain
Spleen
Skin

CB1   Receptors are predominantly found in the brain and nervous system.

CB2   Receptors are predominantly found in the immune cells and peripheral organs.

Conclusion

The *Healing Paws Method* covers only a partial list of conditions that can be helped with Reflexology. If you know of a preexisting condition that is not covered in the book, just look on the main charts for the point that corresponds to the afflicted part of the body and press the point for as long as your pet lets you. If your pet resists you touching its paws, you can do it while it sleeps. You do not need to press hard or deep. A light touch will do.

There is a subtle energy in Reflexology that almost always achieves positive results. As long as you are on the right spot and you stay there long enough, health improves. One cannot say that Reflexology is the cure-all or end-all for every disease. However, if your pet has a proper diet, space to move around, lots of love and attention from its master, then your pet will respond positively to a good Reflexology session.

There are so many factors that can afflict a pet. Genetic weaknesses, stress, poor nutrition, loneliness, lack of space and insufficient love are just a few. So when working with your animal, be sure to keep this in mind.

It is my hope that these simple techniques outlined in this book will significantly help and improve the quality of your pet's health. There are numerous alternative approaches gaining momentum in the world of animal health and every one of these alternatives is worthy of exploration. Reiki, massage, Acupuncture, homeopathic remedies and herbal treatments, all of these can bring relief. Any of or a combination of these holistic therapies can be applied with excellent results. You may combine alternative approaches with conventional medicine and achieve even greater results.

Presently, many pet lovers are reporting vast improvements in the health of their animal from the use of cannabinoids, a hemp plant derivative better known as CBD. CBD is not psychoactive and does not have any cannabis ingredients that cause the sensation of being high, specifically THC. CBD has been proven safe and effective in clinical testing.

I have seen Reflexology help so many. Its power to heal never ceases to amaze me. While my focus once was primarily with people, my work with animals has shown me that they too can be helped by this wonderful and simple healing technique. Once you have applied Reflexology to your pets, you will see for yourself what I have witnessed and I do not doubt that you too will become a believer and a proponent of Pet Reflexology. You might even find yourself buying a book on Reflexology for humans and applying it to yourself, your friends and members of your family!

Always remember that in the final analysis, it is the love you share with your pet that makes the greatest difference. Reflexology will put in your hands the power to transform your love into a healing tool which will significantly enhance your pet's quality of life throughout the many and meaningful years of your friendship. Good luck and happy paw rubbing to everyone who applies the principles of the ancient healing art of Reflexology!

Enjoy a long, happy and healthy life with your beloved animals and never lose sight of this amazingly simple yet effective healing tool that is truly at your fingertips.

Thomas Acosta, M.R.

Your furry best friend loves your touch.
Start using the Healing Paws Method. It's simply pawsome!

About the Author

Thomas Acosta is a certified Master Reflexologist. When Acosta discovered that Reflexology works just as well on dogs and cats as it does on humans, he embarked on a mission to share his findings through his book *Healing Paws Method*. Acosta believes Reflexology is the holistic wave of the future; that it's safe, effective and anyone can apply it.

Born in New York City, Acosta began his professional career as a journalist for the award-winning weekly newspaper *The Bronx Times Reporter*, covering hard-news stories and writing editorials. He was the editor of the *Chandler Independent* in Chandler, Arizona and editor of *The Sedona Times* in Sedona, Arizona. He is also the publisher of *Sedona's Best Visitor's Guide*, a publication serving the needs of tourists visiting Sedona and northern Arizona.

Acosta studied Reflexology and achieved his certificate of mastery under the tutelage of Laura Norman, widely recognized as the nation's foremost Reflexologist. Subsequently, Acosta founded

the *New Canaan Institute of Reflexology and Holistic Health* in Connecticut, teaching others the intricacies of the art.

His clients included several famous individuals such as former New York City Congressman Mario Biaggi, fashion designer Eli Tahari and Eric Butterworth, world-renowned Unity minister, radio personality, motivational speaker and author of *Discover the Power Within You*.

Acosta was also a Reflexology instructor at the *Southwest Institute of Healing Arts*, one of Arizona's most prestigious holistic health learning centers. Presently, Acosta continues teaching Reflexology for pets through webinars and instructional videos.

"The path to health and relaxation lies at your feet. Step into our hands, and we'll show you the way."

HAPPY TAILS TO YOU!

#HEALINGPAWSMETHOD

HEALINGPAWSMETHOD.COM